# THE PAST

ALSO BY WENDY XU

•

*Phrasis* (2017)
*You Are Not Dead* (2013)

# THE PAST

## WENDY XU

•

*Wesleyan University Press*
*Middletown, Connecticut*

Wesleyan University Press

Middletown CT 06459

www.wesleyan.edu/wespress

2021 © Wendy Xu

Manufactured in the United States of America

Typeset in Arnhem by Eric M. Brooks

Library of Congress Cataloging-in-Publication Data

NAMES: Xu, Wendy, 1987– author.

TITLE: The past / Wendy Xu.

DESCRIPTION: Middletown, Connecticut: Wesleyan University Press, [2021] |
Series: Wesleyan poetry | Summary: "Poetry that investigates significations
of 'the past' by relating the author's own migration from China to the U.S. to
the 1989 Tiananmen Square protests" — Provided by publisher.

IDENTIFIERS: LCCN 2021015316 (print) | LCCN 2021015317 (ebook) |
ISBN 9780819580450 (cloth) | ISBN 9780819580467 (trade paperback) |
ISBN 9780819580474 (ebook)

SUBJECTS: LCGFT: Poetry.

CLASSIFICATION: LCC PS3624.U7 P37 2021 (print) |
LCC PS3624.U7 (ebook) | DDC 811/.6 — dc23

LC record available at https://lccn.loc.gov/2021015316

LC ebook record available at https://lccn.loc.gov/2021015317

5 4 3 2 1

*opens the book*

*the words have decomposed*

*the ruins have imperial integrity*

- BEI DAO

# CONTENTS

# COMING TO AMERICA

Speak first of the flooded interior, supernaturally lit

          I is an echo in the word

A proximity, birds over land: *exquisite*
A word I've welded into love

          Sure, I was blessed at birth and have outpaced
                 myself gently
They spoke to me in heavy abstraction
My tongue fading out
Sometimes a mouth is lost to slow time

          Did I hear that somewhere?

A gasp of memory appearing now as skin
          I had been looking for something
               in others — a likening
               further inquiry of the lyric self

When something inside me sprung up new, green even
More hostile, less wounded

          How can this be the case?

What can I do, except continue to demonstrate love?

Revision is a practice of faith

Revision is a practice of my love against time

# PLEDGE

## MY DISSENT AND MY LOVE
## ARE WOVEN INSIDE ME

I commune with the text by way of railing against the text
The molecular processes of you are never finished
I move through air in the early fall, a cooling spittle, high heat days are gone
When the troops leave the replica city, you see that its battlements are written
    in green
A Western style of defense, no birds, all men
Same plaza, white stones, black columns, no memory
You want to walk along the path meant for military vehicles and are denied
You want to try falling down where others had before you, and are
    unceremoniously denied
You wanted permission to travel to the mainland to see your mother
All of your desires were completely impractical
That is, you did not want to atone for anything you had done

# LOOKING AT MY FATHER

It's the inside which
comes out, as I contemplate
him there half
in sunlight, weeding diligently
a Midwestern lawn.
On my persons, I have
only notes
and a drying pen,
the memory
of onion blossoms
scenting
in a window.
Reflection is my native
medium. I am never
arriving, only speaking
briefly on material
conditions between myself
and others. My country
inoculates
me lovingly, over time.
My country grasps me
like desire.
I will show you
my credentials, which is
to say my vivid description
if you ask.
Here we are, my father
and I, never hostile,

a small offering: pointless
cut flowers appear
on the kitchen table
when one
finally arrives
into disposable income.
Still possible.
Am I living? Do I
accept revision
as my godhead
and savior? I do
and I am, in the name
of my Chinese father now
dragging the tools
back inside, brow
shining but always
a grin, faithless
except to protect whatever
I still have time
to become,

Amen.

# A SOUND NOT UNLIKE A BELL

In the dream last night I was desperately arranging cut flowers for something
    important
The practical uses of my work I was not made aware
Nobody was available to assist
Thus the flowers were strewn about the carpet beside me
I was compelled to finish my task by something greater than myself
The forces that acted upon me seemed to say "Your life depends upon this
    assemblage"
I took it as a warning, though provocative, though urgent and abstract
The bouquets were to be picked up as soon as I declared them finished
I admit, it felt good to be the lone member of mission control
There's no point in talking of how time passes in a dream; I worked for minutes
Perhaps I worked for years
The only accompanying sound was a song looping in my mind about the little
    sparrow
A Chinese folk song from somewhere, the past
I was so alone in my freedom to choose, but because I was under deadline, duress
I did not dare make a mistake
After some time, I stepped away from my work and admired the results
The outcome was beautiful, and because I had worked very hard: *rare*


•


We don't remember how we got here, so have woven a beautiful story of
    replacement
You mispronounce my sacred name, always in front of others, there it goes
A fine white mist where once it held space for me
I didn't write for the longest time because you were speaking for me

You had so many eyes trained on you, I wanted them only on me
In order for me to work towards an undoing of my condition, I must know the
    characteristics of my condition
In order for me to know the characteristics of my condition, I must not be made
    to feel alone in my perception of them
You are and have always been subject to randomness
Accept it

•

In World War II the chemical giants (Monsanto, DuPont) made a fortune
    through exclusive government contracts to spray death from above
If you think about it for too long you will feel hysterical
You will point erratically at the audience in a frenzied female state
You will stare at the miniature hurricane of Liquid Plumber spiraling down
    towards the clog like a heavy godsend

•

Poems of the deadpan subject
Poems of the habitually deferred
Poems of the yellow hand and matching face
Poems of the song that feels like a secret
Poems of the fancy free
Poems of the who and what do I love now with all this money?

•

I had felt the similes falling away from my holy body
In sharp relief and judgment of you, who have yet to recognize me
I wanted disgusting excess for my family this year, my food out of your mouth
But my practice was of looking at the image and conjuring it up from the
    margins

I was crying there in the great hall like something I had never felt

It was repugnant to words

You had your eyes trained on me crying in church

I was tired of being worn by you like fashion and hungry for my life to begin

I attempted to face the successes of those around me


•


Pedestrian thoughts again about the body in recovery

Fragile clock, weak and porous until suddenly in revolt

All these days stuck alone at home

Parents in the world are like a roving evaluation, never knowing where their
    gaze will fall

On the mouse emerging from the wall

On the wall itself, in need of repair

A friend says "My accent never fails to make them laugh" and I catch myself
    laughing

Then laugh again at the brilliant entrapment

The completion of a closed unintentional loop

Lost to laughter now, unable to suck it back into my body

I read a testimony about the loneliness of large unfilled spaces and sense my
    parents preparing to board the plane now

Little pleasures of my own: burping, fruit


•


Your historical loveliness knows no bounds

Who is Tank Man to you?

My what if and my thank god

Tank Man torn apart by my would-be friends

Tank man dancing immortal as GIF

Tank Man as where you stop reading

Tank Man has been around the world but not back

Tank Man as nobody you care to know

I left and I admit I did not turn around, how could I, I was still shitting in my
    diaper

Every June I look around and you are ordering Tank Man, I am reunited with
    him on your plate

The day passes over you with grease on its wings

It was a luxurious silence, then a long sleep in the margins where my family
    owns a plot

Things as they are are inexorable

Time felt absolute and came back to humiliate me

I acknowledged language, my untrustworthy friend

A consideration of my new home was anatomical and of many parts I was
    ashamed

Filled with an abstract grief

Tank Man doesn't care about your velveteen ideas of protest

Tank Man finally on vacation on Martha's Vineyard

Tank Man declining to be killed by you just a few more times

Tank Man as a cosmology of fetishized suffering at the center of the world

I had said to people "Isn't it funny"

If I am a social animal, I say much more or much less


•


Last night on the phone, bored to death while Dad live-translates my new
    poems into Chinese

He probes the meaning behind phrases until I think "You just don't get it"

Later he explains to me the metrics of Chinese classical verse and I think "I just
    don't get it," and we laugh together

A sound not unlike a bell

It is beautiful to please one's parents

Though somewhere it is written that piety is neither interesting nor progressive


•

Mom tells me a story: an immigrant arrives *here*
Eventually working second shift at a garment factory she saves up enough
    money to purchase a used car
Then she must take a driving test
Then she must secure childcare to travel to the test but cannot afford it
She asks to bring her baby in the car and is granted permission
She is nervous and immediately places the car in reverse
Nearly fails then and there
The roads are covered with ice and you must imagine a brutal winter
It is dangerous for Mom and baby both
Who then, is at fault?
If your flight lands at JFK but the shuttle leaves from LaGuardia
And you must take a bus with your four rolling suitcases and baby
It's not that you are afraid, but something entirely more particular
An ache that moves frequently and with greater purpose

•


Flowers carried on an invisible hand above the ocean, color peeling off of me
Ruled by Chinese astrology, which is to say mood, I eat the mooncake to
    prepare for the new year
My sadness supplements my vision when I write
A factory where I reproduce myself daily, go nonverbal
Like beach trash and unanswered questions

•


Suppose I oppose the corporate merger of DuPont and Dow Chemical
After the merger, the mega company will be re-split into three new entities
One for textiles, one for chemicals, one for agriculture
The third of which employs not one but both of my parents
The layoffs are imminent and the mood in the office is tense

Dad missed his opportunity to transition laterally into academia and we are all
    nervous
Dad has acquired numerous bio-patents over the years, the prestige of which
    will likely allow him to keep his job
He appears in the diversity initiative videos produced by the company
He brings them home on a little flash drive
I pull a knife across the grapefruit's glistening skin and can't bear to watch


•


Admit: that moment in time is completely imaginary
You do not remember nor can you ever
You call it up into being at will
Perhaps we did not even travel to the airport in any hurry or under duress
Perhaps we stopped for lunch in the wide public square
Mom admiring the perfectly manicured azaleas, the trim shrubbery
But it is a fact that there was unrest
Crowds violently dispersed only to reassemble at different points in the city
If we cried, it's difficult to say what we mourned the loss of
There was so much we would not see again for many years
Did we pass through any checkpoints on the way?
Was Dad questioned for his timely departure from the country?
Did they ask him what he studied in Beijing, who he consorted with, his
    political views?
Do you support a democratic upheaval now or have you ever?
Why are you leaving today?
Is the department of molecular biology and research pro-West?
By design or by luck we boarded the plane
I didn't cry once, the sweetest baby on an international flight the others had
    ever seen
Perhaps I became the star of the trip, passengers cooed over my impressive
    calm

Perhaps Mom and Dad cried in lieu of me
I had not yet known about my losing


• 


A wish list:
You who have listed me first
You who follow
You who name me incorrectly
You who do nothing to find me
"You and Yours"
You who would bring up the rear
Your friends
Your enemies
You who would mispronounce me
You especially, saying nothing


• 



Yesterday all I managed to write was a note to myself that read "what is this
      poem even about," and unable to find the poem in question
In the '90s my parents took what jobs they could get
With each paycheck we felt our loneliness coming to an end
Pointless cut flowers began to appear next to the kitchen sink, remember?
I will accelerate into carefree adulthood now, I might have said
A body follows a mind to the edge, and then what?


• 



I need these parameters around my speech
They push on me sensually, and yet I am always still listening for you
I'm too sensitive to receive criticism for longer than moments at a time
Mom says I'm getting too fat, and this is the Chinese way

She says look at your soft white hands

They're perfect she says you are perfect

May you never shove them down firmly into the farmed earth and pull up a root
vegetable

May you never flex them to delay atrophy

May you never sweat in an unbecoming way or see the past the way we
remember

In my last life I was a realist without the constitution for prose

Mom says I am so beautiful and overfed

Look at your smooth pale cuticles and oval nail beds

There is only one lifetime of praise in me, and I have not abandoned nostalgia
just yet


•


I said I would write for her in the new year and send the drafts home in lieu of
money

Unable to find the note that makes me sing, the text repeats my body into
another

Where is the song finally trained upon me?

Not among the neon signage of the street at night

This poem is not for you

I only promised to approach the opening and let my tenses slip generously wide

This is where I come to be alone with words

I belly up to the sentence and live to construct this house for the vocal dead

Can you imagine:

We used to answer the phone to declare our unknowing

"Hello! I do not speak English!"

"Thank you!"

Who, is it you?

Why are you calling?

I echo out miles at a time but not to you

## PRAXIS

I had put down in writing my fear of the war
I too pined for pastoral description
The blue of the water was the blue of the world

       Newness does not, for me, equal satisfaction
       A finite number of concentric rings I push out into space

A tedious fabric moving through time without malice
An act of oration, rebellion, inventory, fantasy

       The sound of the earth closing its one good eye over me
       Imagine: you reach out towards the margin's white hand

You do what your poems want and are clean
When you lay down your thorns you will be done
You do not take up arms against anyone

# WRITING HOME

An absence declares
its blunt self. I can't believe the extent
of my luck, heard twice, like violets
in a bath of lukewarm water.
The city was my father's though none
of its sweetness appears here living
before you. A strong instrument.
A blowing on the hands
and neck. A curtain almost open.
I inherited a stiff collar sewn
against loveliness where once
we must have walked freely into
the city square and gathered
there like intention. Two lips bloomed
on my mother's cheek. I felt
a heavenly peace. Here, the marker you
might have waited for: ancient
dough, rolled and fried. These days
the lyric's sentiment floats
away from me, like a river someone
forgets to bless. Memory, to memory
to the dirt path opening
again in a dream. I have not been back
for many years. I walk the distance
in my mind, the margins flowing by
like so much foreign water.

# NAMES OF THE RIVER

I did wrong by all ideas of *nation*, haunted
by the after-
                        life of speech, public acts wagging
their dutiful tails
I sat down
in the crosswinds of a feeling, too wild
                        to write it out how the velcro parts
of me unstuck themselves

                        But do you too, alone, ever
feel incompetent? If in one hand holding
a wet tissue for dignity
                        when the Yangtze view
leaves you cold?
Somewhere in America a white boss
in a dandelion dress-shirt is raising
his voice again
                        A quick pivot to the page where
I stare down the verbs and am afraid
to make a recitation of myself—
                        am I *unimitable*, or, is this just another feeling?

By all accounts the river
was yellowed over time, a yolk
        running over land, and yet in places:
                        pearly foam, like clouds
like the overlook I might
have photographed, sinewy green and the snow-
                        pricked thumb
                        of that mountain
                        (I've forgotten
                        its name)
                        under which nobody
                        I still remember
                        to call was born
                        in the days when they came
                        and tried to take my mother
                        away in a van
                        to the county hospital
                        for procedures
                        against her will
                        for the good of the population
                        growing too fast
                        because of dumb ugly
                        country folk
                        like her

had the day not been hot
and mean, a government calling me home
        by a different word
I would have made a record of everything
                        there flowing
        from the mouth of the river:

"The Yellow and Deep Water"
"The Big Mouth"
"The Five Stars"
"The Tao"

One reminding me now of the next, heavier
than foreign air,
   their yellow names soaking the page

# THE ECSTASY OF TIME

Begin in texture approaching green, a pause, my condition

repellant to form. Pause again and live

    with the history of me. Spilling over. When you stand

beneath the sentence concentric you disorient

        neon speech. Do you hear me calling from across

ecstatic silence? Along the deep cut trespassed, along linear

    expression I touch my family. A condition of light pours

from a loss in the door. A beetle roams the page

at night, it crosses the inky folds of time. I hear

    ancient speech. Roses laid down white upon the sentence.

A posture. A taste like humming a name.

# LINEAR TRAVEL

Perhaps with nonhuman animals, war is a state of being, an ultimately
natural occurrence. Thus, it cannot be called war. In writing you try your
hand at elegy which suspends the act, person, or event being mourned.
You have seen the list of names and have heard the conclusions.
You follow them anyway on the page. Through time. An evocation of
tenderness which requires knowledge of the departed's interiority.

Did he rush in? Was he fool-headed and eager? Was he in fact reluctant
and carried forth by the epitaph written against his will? Did he love his
children most of all? What did the neighbors have to say of him?

You honor me with your ongoing fearlessness, careful not to discolor
what you believe in with too many examples. When they come for you,
conspire first and most attentively with your dead, make faithful note of
every imagined assertion of self in hostile spaces.

When the self cracked open there inside was a sentence cracking in
tandem. Tell them there was a song in you then.

# FIVE CHINESE VERSES

Music, wind, someone's car horn
Imagining to return
Buddha's big toe on the lake
Your intricate gaze of form

Eating the lake like a word
Unzipped carefully by day
You walked it hesitantly
You taste something step by step

•

Losing my way, wildly blue
Perhaps annotated past
The return gaze, my snowfall
My city gate firmly shut

Even to wonder how you've been
Isn't what you want, therefore
Lightly enclosing my text
Cast down towards what I've not seen

•

Happily a ceiling fan
You grasp the word sweltering
Days are tectonic, the sound
Of one memory spoken

Who waits for you at the lake's
Wild edge? Bright glint of the noun
You knew dissatisfaction
Speaking even against time

•

Recorded lengthening dark
I held memory tightly
Unoriginal dimming
Of the light there, a found scene

Number three on the dirt path
Father carries his school bag
Without use for meter, yet
Both skies open to thunder

•

Don't speak to me of sorghum
Red fields, pressed up toward a sky
Whatever called to me there
Too wild, attempting a face

Old verses for my father
Dignify the cooling page
Black earth is the word it makes
Tilts forward, consequential

# INTERIM POETICS

I walked there guilty by tongue but not by mind

The water was breaking on a soft green rock

The rock was breaking underfoot despite a lack of intention

My works contained no genius, only an agitated bouquet of ideas

White ones, sand ones, some almost blue

By day I moved easily enough through the offices of disappointing money

Uninterrupted, nobody stopped to ask for any music

I knew my family's faces by pinkness and language comprehension

Something like a fond electricity was happening inside of me

I felt I could lay there forever on the tarmac by the sea

A three-legged chair, a clock, a door opening into the ragged surf

My eye passed over without judgment or apprehension

A feeling entered quietly then, through the four walls of my murky inheritance

Just lost in the technicolor thought of it

A brush stroking to the left, a government whistling while it hurts

I receive its washed-up objects and contain not a single word

# PLEDGE

The diagnosis was god, twice a day until the spirit
untangles itself         I took a trip into unscripted
days past, teenagers submit to the window an open
facing yawn        A walnut fell into the grave
of my loved one and stayed there beating patient
like a word       I was still unmoved by disbelief watching
my father mumble the pledge and hot white stars
he can't remember      Nobody got hurt, some un-
fulfilled potential exits the room     Enter, knowledge.
Men came to dispel ambiguity and raced
my intention to a hard boiling over     Each new decade
we stayed was a misinterpretation
of genre      We showed our teeth to those
who would listen    In the face of the absent subject
I felt my desire go flaccid, the leaves fell dutifully one
by one from their limbs    But I wrote to you against
all odds     Money     Paperwork    Love's heavy
open door. Critique. Indignity. Vision and often
enough time.

# INVENTORY FOR SPRING

Feeling rich for one moment for using money as a bookmark

Feeling deceitful for making public some opinions while neglecting others

Feeling disordered at the sight of three statues conspiring in a row

Feeling insufficient for having a lukewarm reaction to the news

Feeling important for having been offered a seat at the table

Feeling apologetic for nonetheless tuning out an argument

Feeling blue for identifying some people who don't respect you

Feeling like a knife slipping into a pool of water for bearing disagreement

Feeling redundant for moving in a similar direction as others

Feeling angry for imagining the opening of the passage yet unopened for you

Feeling antisocial for declining further missives from home

# RESIDENT ALIEN

A clump of heavy-hearted clouds attempting to sound. Pink ennui
was my accomplice. The moon, the mind, the resentful storefronts I
visited, snuffed out like rogue winter flowers. In this future, I was truly
inconsolable.

Questions arose into the blue: from which housing block? Is the
cable box bought and paid for? Every night, a demented field of black
grasshoppers, the letters arrived with dirt in their delicate seams.

Nobody was available to make a translation of the signs. Shore to
lavender waves. On some days I forced out ugly new words from the gut.
I counted them like pearls scattering across a stranger's table. A mask of
air was all I wore, and yes, I lived to serve their translucent glow.

# TWENTY-FIRST CENTURY WORDS

In our language the sweetness
of sugar mirrors *heaven*, but the tonal edge
slopes up gently, there and away
from my small attempts at public-
facing speech. First a wet jaw
clicking open, then back down and *I*
emerges out of myself, don't I?
The pair of girls was laughing
in the tea shop, oolong and gunpowder
      *China green*, the sound aspiring
            to evidentiary music but the jasmine
                  takes no milk, won't froth the way you like.
              I could relate to you with something
            other than a pledge, but you're a whole-
        ass nation, you may be sick by now
with impatience, you and all
your friends humming steadily along.
You were so obvious
almost exquisite. There was nothing
inelegant to say, not a wound nor
opening to make, just the lowly
murmur of a threat hung quietly
      between us. Impossible to the tongue,
        I know. For the eye alone.

# READING THE CANON

A word parts like obedient water
along the milky seam
of its own destruction
       Fumbling into tonal valleys green
with your delight

I'm not there, scaling the memories
of my own country word
          by jagged word
Footfalls on the tongue's
      unfamiliar stairs, like ambush

Or worse? Soft exterior stained
with accommodation
     But
there was a poem I once mis-
remembered, about the chinky Chinaman

      who delivers the news
      Flare of his foreign nostrils
         Pink unsoothing lips
            Moody intelligence of the poem's
own face as it regards him

      Does he have a soul?
The poem's curiosity flickers, illuminates,
         dulls and kneels, negotiates

itself to death

Please, Mr. Chinaman was my father

You can call me something all-
                together new:

Unlucky heirloom, an eager match
struck on the lips
Both lips struck against the curve
        of the sound and its vicious hollow

Alien words and the velocity
                    in all directions
with which they find you

# LOOKING BENEATH THE SENTENCE'S WING; 1989

What I saw there;

the grasses streams trees
rivers stones mountains
      the pale orange crystal pulled from the rock face
      the wayward clots of white and lavender clouds

luminescent jellyfish
      the inlet crisscrossed by birds

the silver sheen of water
      children marking it with fists
and winds unbound by municipal borders sheltering me
                *tender heartedly*
needle-nose pines in a damp field stinging the air
      covetous old knots on a string
            still tied to my grandfather's big toe in Shandong
rough and green flowers falling
in a long tradition
over his body
      and my father straining his red-tipped ears
      towards an American middle ground
the dark sermon of those early years      crisis of distance
      and wild power of my mother —

      wild new discipline that nonetheless held
         back feverishly her tongue

# LOOKING BENEATH THE SENTENCE'S WING; 1999

That first decade of golden-haired complaints passed quickly
                  beneath our rusted awning

Subterranean floor
    where the immigrants go

Some years still tugging (how like our parents) now at my coat strings

Blue wash and deep blue waves mapping hands

    Or the signature lines where I wrote my former
             un-impounded name     like wrongfully accused
                                  inks of the past
Diurnal blossom of opportunity
    a shade of moth-winged salon pink: "Rice Rice Baby"
          that my mother    wouldn't paint
          my mother       dying her grays along the seam
                       unbreaking her English

For the one century down     impossible
                    Another to go

# AFTER IS NOT RETURN

Outside the old house,
        concrete aging
away from me: three men
in green jackets, dark hair
patching a sidewalk

Set the scene and do not
yet undo it (let it move
in the direction
of time: silence
        to sight,
        to inevitable
        speech
        to mood)

How many fathers past
and ambitious sons?
A blue parakeet singing
from the neighbor's
gridded roof (escaped
        from a cage at market)

Human words
move me towards
confession (memory a slim
            blade slipping
                    the apple)
cuts towards unintended
            flesh instead

The air was full of listening wires
            buzzing for names

When I was once a private person
and wish
to be again (says the poem
            fearing judgment)
I walked (past the heavy red
            torches of sorghum)
and when I tried        to stop
I tried and
tried
and I could not

# DESCRIPTION, REPETITION

The scenes whizzing by, threaten to coalesce
I'm prone to granular thought but accept their sincerity:

the garden rose trimmed in black, like the death of a thought
There goes the whim, the whiff, of a passing

remembrance, its dazzle just overhead
The two of us trespassing the paid gardens and that day

I longed for it, the afternoon boldly flickered first white
then ripening pale yellow, blush, the speech of a pear in technicolor

In a dusty room with sleeves off, casually in repose your lines
against the window, tidying an old notebook

One foot on the cat, inscriptions plucked in their entirety
from a mysterious wind

What was it again that I and everyone else wanted yesterday?
Expensive Asian ceramics that never chip

Slim necks, silver curving for the thumb's touch
Something else I've forgotten: where the *word* goes

# TIANANMEN SONNETS

Tiananmen "6 x 4" sonnets contain 14 lines:

6 lines of 4 words

4 lines of 6 words

4 lines of 4 words

they are built to evade algorithmic censorship

of the numbers 6, 4, 89,

and other references to ███████████

Dead air in air
The anniversary of language
holds you back against
bucolic dreaming, down stream
from *here* is running
a miraculous color, elegy

bursts like a ribbon in air
Thinking again of the Square today
Bold sky, passing episodes of cloud
Vegetation mutters in the Far West

A column of ghosts
going violet over time
Familiar song looping overhead
Lines pressed in air

Stems of the lily
Of the plum blossom
Pink heads knocked around
on a windblown day
*Wind swept the square*
*Who swept like wind?*

Champagne burst from the cannon's mouth
Like touching the pearl of history
in a poem, the unnatural shell
nonetheless does its duties to form

The parade of emperors
in sashes appeared just
at blue black dusk:
watched another year explode

Flight attendants are kind
to the Chinese baby
wrapped in petroleum fleece
(Tragedy or a lamb)
Goodbye to cow country,
the green peaches kissed

by immortal blush — fragrant new century
teasing you from behind white clouds
Just down below some protestors disappear
during beverage service, *gone so soon*

whispered in a hush
Not life but deathlessness
Stones in a river
River mapping white palms

Some who warble on
dotingly about the past
achieve a monosyllabic yellow
Asking what's possible or
what's dead, running through
the mind's most urgent

refrain: *I am not always dissatisfied*
By starlight sowing the rich field
of discontent, rainwater falling between lines
Remembrance annoys the cat (two paws

against history) snoring there
in a moon-silvered window
Best to leave her
happy — humbler than most

Surface of jade troubled
slow by veining white:
the past doesn't remember
its hysterical color moving
freely out, who now
is tame, whose death-

defying passage was noiseless and clean?
I stood blinking in the Square
Myself a perimeter of unloved critique
All was sound and the beep

of a censor waking
to its never-ending work —
Ragged length of shadow
whispering softly to itself

*After Wang Wei's "Thinking of My Brothers*
*East of the Mountain"*

She conjures an evicted
memory, playing across windproof
computer screens just once:
*Heavy willow blossoms trailing*
*water green as jade*
Among the rarified landscapes

of grief, everyone shuffles to be found
West of Wang Wei's poem see
brothers stranded in the apricot mist
Their feet stitched on land, simulating

mountain, village, dull nation —
And if they're missing
in inaction, forgive them
Their useless pearls, nouns

Pigeons crowd the air
A white silk gown
of clouds, heir apparent
to "doors of opportunity"
Preparing the good ink
to write: *yesterday Uncle*

*has died,* before him died another
Now gathered into a single country
with ugly known boundaries, grief rides
a breeze across the velvet sea

Determined to live substantially
Description pollutes the past
with color: cinnamon, sterling
Memories racing against red

*In my little office on the ground floor, feeding the stapler another cartridge*

*Dust nibbling my forearms*

*The screen emits a glow sickly fluorescent, or it's my own face*
*that's yellow, the light just truth-telling*

*Thirty years this June, when I almost was not*
*and suddenly: was, but I do not salute the past*

*There are no windows unto it, save one, an object of amnesiac refusal:*
windows of history, open up

*No, just another room half-shaded, full of someone else's belief*

*To give a sense of seconds passing, like light at the end of the day*
 *crumbles from the air*

*All its unfulfilled conditions*

*I imagined a form that would preserve the shape*
*of the column of tanks from my recurring dream*

*Their grays and smoke, their outlines, the force of their intentions*
*in all possible directions*

*Punching through time*

*A form for "the past itself" is an idea*

*Too elegant to exist, is a compartment I can't keep*

> *When rarely and at best, I would show you the room*
> *that the dissolving letters make*

> *The weight of the day passing through it*

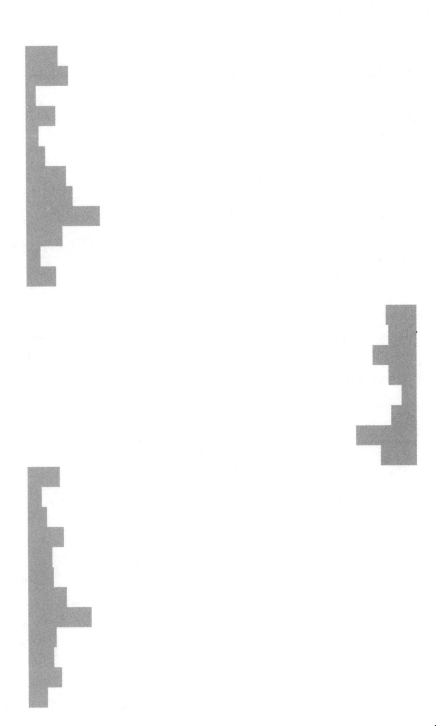

51

Blossom
Pink
*the*
*square*
unnatural
duties
appeared

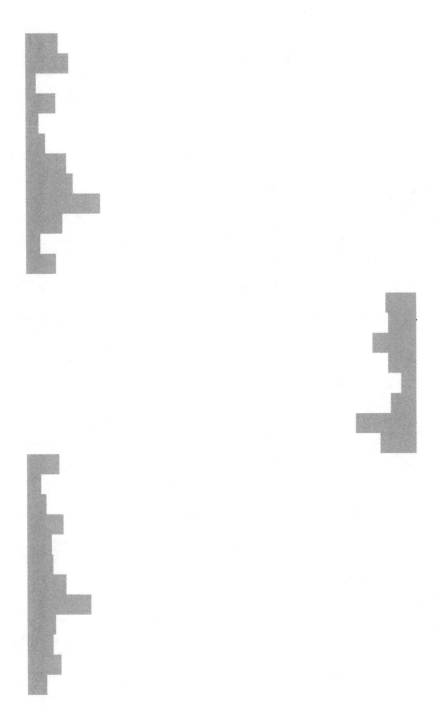

53

Dead
language
back
dreaming
miraculous
ribbon
of
the
West

doors
of
ink
before
him
died
known
boundaries
grief
with
color:
red

dotingly
yellow
not
always
sowing
between
lines

once:
grief
shuffles
West
on
land
simulating
nouns

57

green
immortal
century
hush
but
deathless

white
moving
is
tame
in
the
Square
unloved
never-ending
length
of
itself

# THE PAST

# A POEM ON MY MOTHER'S BIRTHDAY

Trees singing a suburban dark call me back home, forgetting time to
mine for dignity in the poem's acid core. Just a wound rejecting air and
ointment alike. Young starlings in the seeded grass, rabbits, Eastern
beetles leaving their brittle skins behind on the lawn: young and old at
once, her sorrow thick and milk-white.

Uncle has passed, and Uncle before him, Uncle of the wind tipping
baskets of squash blossoms from the balcony's ledge, blossoms on the
neighbor's patchwork roof, lifting with summer air, without regard for
melancholy, for death which follows speech but does not undo it, for the
chlorine that crept into Uncle's bones and stayed, greening there.

The cake doesn't taste like home at all, and she cuts its scalloped layers
with her good arm, the other sleeps in its sling, it thunks and hurts
her at night. We eat exchanging soft permission to touch the future,
mysterious diurnal flower of existence, its irresistible center. I sing
Happy Birthday. Hold her in ecstatic outline.

# LIST OF FORGIVENESSES

The children I was, the chemical-bitten
green of their sadness, who watched

the generational assembly of prior
knowledge, whose shame formed somewhere

over the neon ocean. Sorrow is ever
inelegant, the squat concrete faces

that greeted them. Not knowing where
to pass the salt at endless

Christian tables. Whose hand to hold,
whose tongue, yearlings stalking

the wilted margins of America.
Light through trembling fingers

of foreign trees. Who once cut
their hair tight-black and straight

across the forehead. Whose blood
was dark as soy, vinegared

cabbage, radish root.
The hours adrift in someone's

blue eye, the humble light
that carried them there.

The tragedies I thought I was.
The slow burn of moonlight

each night, up there patiently
unbelieving even in itself.

# POEM ABOUT MY LIFE

The opening to another country was always inside
my father's mind, in many forms, in dreams: green swords

swirling in a winter mist, colorful moths, sometimes
a molar falling out, porcelain clattering onto the table

like a single rung chime. When I come into the house I am held
by him, become a child again. The view from here seems

never to change, but in wishing it, over many years,
I have changed it. A new worry is my father's

more delicate footsteps picking out a path to the bathroom sink
at night. The hair beneath a gardening hat leaking its color.

When the writing will not come then I must go
to the porch and listen there to the talking of one tree

to its double, and think of my father, who used to say that living
is not so painful as living would have

you believe. When as a teenager I borrowed the rusted Nissan,
drove it through a field and returned it to him with sudden

blue flowers tucked into its mouth. The bluest one
he saved. The wind that made those dull trees sing, blowing in

from the future. Somewhere my father has never been.

# WANG XIN TAI SAYS GOODBYE

Some things are not so plain to say, that I
am sometimes in pain and occasionally sit
to write my name in dark inks and the brush
goes wobbly, as if excited into shapes
without me. The crop fields of someone's childhood
still bother the edges of my vision, tawny
gridded country, lowborn, wind gripping the assembled
heads of wheat, bristling. One job seems now
just like another. I was a worker in a factory,
a prison, other places ill-defined. But I remember best
the war, the American G.I.'s. They taught me
my English swears, whole rooms cleared of men
and dogs as I cursed them up and down, my hand
on my little lieutenant's hip, the green
and the muddy browns. In this life I even crossed
the ocean in an airplane, drank too many coca-colas
on the flight, ordered with flashcards
I stored beneath my hat. It wasn't profound.
At the end, your life doesn't really churn before your eyes.
It's not a colossus that plays itself back
upon the eyelids like a final prayer. But the soda
was good, sweet. It popped and sang
on my tongue like English, someone remembering
me in the present tense.

# GŪ DĀN

Means loneliness bound
to a single language
Many-crested hills blooming
vernacular seafoam

The confusion of small once-
connected things

Tides upheaving a shore
Blue shot through skin

Cylinders of spun concrete
and their dusty tails trailing behind

A little bit of peace this morning:
some stitches in the word
held you together

Families with children
on their way to the public library
stop to watch the trapeze man
dangling from pink satin ropes

What's bad is writing
without the feeling to write
You disappear from the road
where we have walked together many years
The illnesses, the breath
mastered by illness
The body inside the breath

What all this writing becomes:
a helicopter parting two clouds
catches you alone refusing
to speak against yourself

# A DREAM OF SHANDONG

Fog grasping concrete
Some trees babbling into air

Why do I turn my head piously
to the sky?

Cranes of steel
and smoke were opening
their hungry beaks

Little sorrows arranged
on the stove top at home:
        pills for Grandfather
        Uncle's tank of air

Cords of dust traveling
mischievously into corners
while I spin around
on a rock of my own invention

a servant to the black and white cat
that hooks into my shirt-sleeve
Her lavish ambivalence

I come here to think
and eat up another sky

To sit with Uncle
unbothered for a day
in the shade of a maidenhair tree

Discouraging intention
like a brand new thing
Nothing at all dark or lonesome
when he wakes

I write land-shy words to Uncle
as soft as mute wind
sailing across the tops of his hair

## ELEGY FOR SOFT THINGS

The green ache like crescendo up
across the cheek, hugs the wincing eye —
            unsolvable as this Wednesday's metallic rain
                silver and burning
                as a factory's insides

Some hours I laid there like the dead in a shady corner
or in the bathroom mirror
            fingering that shyest molar
A miniature district of pain

Birds continued to shit from the air into uncovered manholes
An ugly haircut on television decried trees

When I looked across the table at my love
            he was saying something about the president
About the koi in the disappearing meadow
            and the needs of children we won't have

The twinkle in my eye was beginning to hurt again

I'll be there soon to recline in the chair
                while they mix up the heavenly white paste
with a plastic knife
Tip the concrete into my mouth as if I too
            were a city in need of hardening

## POEM BEGINNING TO SOUND

Myself as echo, failed synonym
        Disappeared music returns to my father's house
playing against a white painter's cloth nailed to the wall

        (a flag was waving distantly)
           (the perimeter wet with flowers)

Like a child burying favorite words in the sandbox
        I filled the undying year with tasks
           (I keep at it)
Planting fingers in the gaps between lines
I wrote notes into an opening
        for he who departed in color, I knew only lightly

        (across from the oil-filling station, rosettes of cloud)

It's Saturday and I've made promises to remember the dead

        Some circuitry ticking painfully in the forehead now that Uncle is gone

A needlework of electrical wire passing
           through the young heads of trees
Old books begin to bore me, their yellowing answers
Birds squawking poetry beside a rusty pond

and Uncle in my mind turning always
        like the last abundant word

## POEM FOR FEELING'S SAKE

Morning with a feeling to walk
Limbs churning through air and the traffic so polite

Where the past meets the day's magnetosphere
a hectic body, growing older and more unknown
                as the mood turns

Trees in the plaza boxing for sky
Something dry and melancholy rustling underfoot

I passed the sunburned outline of a vine against the garden's pale wall
One bud in the neighbor's gutter
                the other reaching as it opens

Who am I to think about philosophy, money?
Reading books
When the color of the hour was really gemstone chiffon
                swirling in a giant god's eye

When time coughed me up naked and dazzling
I was hungry for nectarines and heavy cream
Fish heads in broth, sprouted white beans

While up from here, past a cool starry nothingness:
                infallible satellites roaming in description

        their chrome rabbit-ears tweaking out human signs

# POEM FOR CHORES

*for Jon*

Today his esophagus aches
The words choking a little inside their tubes
       and swishing the blue soap
around yesterday's bowl, light hums the attendant
seams of dust —

He coughs twice
into a shirt sleeve, the cat rustles
       and shreds her papers
The mouse in the tub he released
with a blessing: until next time

In the interim the To-Dos in neon
       went on and on

In the mind, terrain of neurotransmitters
       or cobwebs? Stopping at the desk
to pluck an unripe word
Each day he sits down with the sun
       whispers to his lime
           as he muddles

Sweeps the broken glass to safety

Polishes the chrome bits

I look for him there at the end
of a task: his pinky finger curled
up just so

       A hook, or the enchanting sail
of his hand
now at rest

The comma before the rest of him

# BREACH SONG

Punctuated by objects of death / now looking around the room / eyelet, cream
      To ask why be known / invent guttural grammar / a voice from the past
            says surface

Is one way to live / floating on a bed of rose droppings

Sunlight troubling the dusty etceteras / the eye / roams further / organic
      structures move
            Across its surface / the eye is the point / the eye desiccated by time

Photograph of Uncle / mass of yellow, green embrace / infinity of the eye
      shuttering open

When my love repeats itself whole / massed like foam / vomit on bleached tile /
      words got wet
            Escaping the mouth / not all who fled entered the next room

The past was decapitated / firing through syllabic air escapes
            The body two ways / becomes the same old red data / quintessentially
                yourself

Until death / do you depart

# WHY WRITE

Uncle visits me in the film where the artist encounters a dead man in the park, unconvincingly half-hidden in the bushes, and the chance to photograph death is so electric and brief that the artist runs away, forgetting the camera and the dark hum of the trees at night, runs to find a buyer for the photograph he has already forgotten to take.

Uncle belongs to the airlessness of memory, soft and black and quiet, while I hold to the white of the page, its paling folds, a skiff charging the future, cargo-less, tired. Were it any other color. Uncle doesn't take sides now that he is dead, or he is forever on the side of the dead, who collect their prize every time. I am writing to reach the winning side.

Uncle expels doubt from the sentence threatening to double back on itself, its anger at carrying forth in a mute direction, its grief over where it began. Uncle begins again, while I pluck a memory at random, tender as it is: clear onion stew, from which Uncle ladles up a single unlidded goat's eye, laughs and begins to see us with it. The squealing of children for more, the living oblige. I am not writing to photograph the past. I am writing to sit inside the pauses of Uncle's sentences, the commas of the dead.

The stormless harbor where Uncle rests his head.

# NOTES FOR AN OPENING

Time is very interesting in an academic sense
In a lived sense it is the most boring thing in the world
What do I observe, internalize, "move on" from, regret, jest at, forgive, invite?
My family gathers in the courtyard without me
They scrutinize my usage of the language I labored to acquire
"I hate to lose" is what I say to the Bank of America fraud consultant

I wanted to craft a more outstanding mode of engagement with the soul
To get children to finish their dinners say "children in Asia are starving"
Is more like "at points my family has been starving"
I relate to my friend that third world factory work is not an abstraction
My family name has held the position for years

•

He describes a moon made of iron, a nail he swallows
It unsettles me because he is many people that I know, except they are not yet
    dead
*He is not an abstraction*
When I describe this to my friend, my friend is intensely interested
    in applying pressure to the context of the poems' writing, how much
    the tragedy skews our appreciation of the craft of the poems themselves
I am unable to see how it is not all the poem
I begin to feel trapped inside the tower of white Western intellectual
    consideration
I feel sick, and worse, "misunderstood"

•

I don't want to be called the other female Chinese poet's name anymore
Or if I am mistaken for the other female Chinese poet, I want a long
    apology in the moment of the recognition of the mistake
What I resent most is the punitive sensibility this is breeding inside me

•

Hunger for some immunity against desire
Which is itself a ferocious desire replicating itself across screens
My desire is to achieve, produce, consume, succeed
My desire perhaps is to be regarded while I undertake this process over time

Fear of the loss of my white allies
Or is it, fear of my white allies

•

I have long fantasized about writing a book called *The View from Here*

People talk about the human condition as infinitely stable

The view from the present condition

I find myself respecting others up to the threshold at which I personally begin to
    suffer

Infinitely separated from them in the moment of our supposed unity,
    bearing witness to spontaneous acts of nature (bay, dolphins) or
    personal disaster (lost phone)

A self-muting (or is it mutilating) lexicon

I do not like crowds, mandatory participation, enclosed spaces

Time is absolutely boring and violent

•

And yet often: so regrettably heartbroken regarding "things as they are"
Wait for life as it happens
I might revise this in the morning, affected by the various metaphors of weather
When the violin cries, reaches out towards an unsustainable note
I worried over seeming clever or unfeeling
I feel repelled by the present moment
A violation of my religious and spiritual beliefs which dictate a present mind

Enter: an evaluation of this text as poetry
Immediately some distance is expanded, the text leans away

Mostly I aspire to an authentic record of thinking situated firmly in time and
    space
A caveat for the meaninglessness of authenticity, its evaluative impossibilities

•

*I go down to the store for replacement bread*
*They do not have the bread I like, I return home*

A primal selfishness leads me to record this in writing
I too seek the femininity of the open page, a bounty
You love to exist in the historical moment, there beneath
    the red "Pepsi Cola" sign
Corporations aspiring to humanity
I lingered in the nail salon because my manicurist was also
    from Shandong and expressed an interest in speaking with me
    in my native language
Sociolinguistically it is not my native language
Considerations of: what is my "native" language
She paints my nails moth-wing pink
The question of where and among whom do I feel most unabashedly myself
That is, where am I most contrasted with others?
An immigrant dreams of total assimilation as both fantasy and nightmare
The abstraction of my self-remembrance

•

*Evaluation is so boring and relates thus to time*

•

On June 1st, 1989, I was a baby carried on an airplane away
    from Shandong, China, the place of my birth, and it was later
    related to me that during the flight I exhibited supernatural calm
A sense of devotion (submission) to the isolation I would later experience
I have mythologized it to the point of memory
Golf masters do this, alongside prisoners of war: intense visualization
    over time seems to the body as good as lived experience
The imagination is an abstraction
Three days later protestors are massacred in Tiananmen Square and the irony
    of the name of the place seems too cheeky, too perfect to talk about
"The Gate of Heavenly Peace"
My father participated quite fully in "brain drain"
In my adult life I throw up on public transportation
I write "false correlation" on the board and slash it red
Adults at the time said there was something in the air and meant it
    as fully abstract though it is fully literal
What was in the air?

•

The face of the Foxconn worker haunts me in its eerie resemblance to my father's
This depresses me
Have you ever put cucumbers in your water? It tastes exactly the same
You open the document
You highlight what is disagreeable in red, you cut it from the page
You make no incision
You agree strongly with the content but not with the manner of its dissemination
The joke of it was how much it cost and this translation into hours labored

•

Impossible then to locate the burial site of feelings within the body
Nor am I convinced that the seductiveness of reverence for the body is productive
Nevertheless I give myself over to it
(Nevertheless I see in you such "material potential")
Some words here from the speaker last night: your goals for me are oppressive
The roses outside are all pink slumped over in a bucket
    where I regard them and take their picture
What is recorded, how they once were, might have been

Where you cut it, it grows there double
Where you splice the tender shoot sprouts (in its exact location) a twinning of
    branches
This is so beautiful and nonhuman I don't know what to say

•

When I loved you deeply and with abandon I saw you
    as without humanity, as an object turning in place
Thus I may replace, regard, dissolve you
A process of welcome retrograde
A process of my own doubt enacted on the living stage of the real
Could I have related to you better as an "artificial intelligence"

.

Or do I hear, a factory outside

Or do I hear, a family outside

•

Who eats whom
Under which flag?

or

Do not describe any more things to me as "ancient"
You are not allowed behind the high stone wall, the courtyard
And what is beyond it
The snow was coming down outside the window, beneath the sky
Perhaps I wanted to know you prepositionally

How and towards whom can I relate if by relation I diminish myself
I obsess over the problem of space
It is not that necessarily you oppress me, rather that I have come
    to know myself only ever in relation to you and our relationship
    is historical
Let there be no visual representation of me without you
Adjust my gaze so that I may be warm enough to please you

94

•

In a painting: white is the prelude smeared over several figures
I roll an old apple between my hands feeling its rot
What else can I describe to you within the verbal framework "in today's world"
Who is still living in "yesterday's world"?
And who is their president
And what technologies drive their daily operations in the snow-globe of the past

When he attributes to me an unfounded Eastern heritage of *naturalism* I ball my
    fists
Am I a child now and if so who is coming to bring me home

My mother sews your mother's beautiful dresses by hand

I'm not mad about it

I just wanted you to know

•

To honor my mother: "be twice as good as them to be taken half as seriously"
She was pinning up her dark hair with a blue jewel
I was a child maybe, or, I was still bloating up with life inside of her
Here I wish to continue being sentimental and wonder about
    the limits of your suspension of disbelief
No, your suspension of suspicion at my remembrance
Could it be dripping of elegy
Does it violate our contract whereby I approach you as one would a priority


*Do you still feel our friendship opening like an exquisite pink blossom?*




*Are you uncomfortable and if so, why?*

# ANNUAL AIR

God had one look
at you in the yellowing
light of birth
and thought, what?
Only God knows, he thought
*God knows what.*
He thought *this one*
*will command nothing,*
not cut out for it, lying
there like a cracked noun
with the hot air
hissing out.
What noun? God
is the only noun
who knows. When you
were just a word
gaining shape
in your mother's mouth
she waited for
the public bus while
it snowed. See?
The poem about money
and disappointment
writes itself if only
you let it. You let it.
Light sliding off
your pointy interview shoes
until the mind

neatly divides
in two. Where clearly
the folded white page
reads *savor*, in bad
afternoon light you make it any
word you please. Some mornings
you wake up and have missed
your mother's best days
on earth, the crust
of that thought just gently
sizzling off. *Sorry.*
The afterlife of speech
has always been
an emergency. The seed
that breaks apart, takes note
of the burying earth.

# ACKNOWLEDGMENTS

Individual poems and excerpts from this book first appeared in *Academy of American Poets Poem-A-Day*, *Ambit* (UK), *Boston Review*, *Conjunctions*, *Granta*, *Gulf Coast*, *The Lifted Brow*, *Literary Hub*, *The New Republic*, *Ploughshares*, *Poetry*, *Tin House*, and *Triple Canopy*, sometimes in slightly different forms.

The poems "Five Chinese Verses" and "Inventory for Spring" were anthologized in *To Gather Your Leaving—An Anthology of Asian Diaspora Poetry from America, Australia, Europe, and UK* (Ethos Books, Singapore), edited by Boey Kim Cheng, Arin Alycia Fong, and Justin Chia.

The poem "Looking at My Father" was anthologized in *Anthology of Contemporary Women Poets* (Edizioni Ensemble, Rome), edited and translated by Alessandra Bava.

The poem "The Ecstasy of Time" was commissioned by Alvin Tran for a group show of the same name at He Xiangning Art Museum in Shenzhen, China, in 2018, curated by Yuan Fuca and Hu Bin.

The poem "Tiananmen Sonnet [Dead air in air . . . ]" was republished in *Why Are They So Afraid of the Lotus?* co-published by Wattis Institute for Contemporary Art and Sternberg Press.

I'm deeply grateful to the editors, translators, and curators of these projects, for their care and attention.

Among many more who have made this book possible in their various and brilliant ways, thank you especially to Chase Berggrun, Chia-Lun Chang, Timothy Donnelly, Jennifer Firestone, Peter Fong, Peter Gizzi, Jess Grover, Alex Halberstadt, Brodie Miron, Stephanie Elliott Prieto, Brandon Shimoda, Emily Skillings, Suzanna Tamminen, Ocean Vuong, Wendy S. Walters, and Jaclyn Wilson. Thank you to my students at The New School for being in community with me while I wrote these poems, for inspiring me, and teaching me so much about poetry.

To Jon, for every day and all of it, thank you.

Thank you to my family, Baba, Mama, and Cindy, and to those who've already gone on ahead. We miss you. This book is for you.

# NOTES

The epigraph comes from Bei Dao's poem "Composition," translated by Bonnie S. McDougall and Chen Maiping.

10  The fate of the 1989 unnamed protester, "Tank Man," is still unknown and the subject of much speculation, despite his anonymous fame and widely circulated image. In addition to photos of his appearance in Tiananmen Square, several minutes of video footage exist of the encounter. You can view it on YouTube as of this writing.

23  "Five Chinese Verses" utilizes the classical Chinese metrical form of four-line stanzas composed of seven syllables per line.

27  "Pledge" owes a debt to Kenneth Koch's walnut from his poem "To You."

30  In Mandarin Chinese, "heaven" or "sky" is a homonym for "sweet," with the exception of its tonal pronunciation. "Heaven" is first tone, "sweet" is second tone.

31  "Reading the Canon" references (a misremembering of) "The Morning of the Poem" by James Schuyler, and the "chinky Chinaman" that does, in fact, appear in Schuyler's poem.

34  "Rice Rice Baby" is a nail polish color by OPI, part of its "Tokyo Collection."

41–61  The figure of each gray "tank" is an erasure made from its corresponding Tiananmen Sonnet, and when in formation appears as either inactive (gray) or active (flashing its inner text).

48  The line "windows of history, open up" owes a debt to Bei Dao's memoir, entitled *City Gate, Open Up* (New Directions, 2018).

69  Wang Xin Tai was my maternal grandfather, who passed away in 2018. As a young man he learned a variety of English swears and

curses from American soldiers stationed in Shandong Province, and delighted in saying them for the rest of his life.

80 "Why Write" references the film *Blowup* by Michelangelo Antonioni, starring David Hemmings.

82 Xu Lizhi (1990–2014) worked in a Foxconn factory before his suicide at age twenty-four. A selection of his poetry was translated into English and published on libcom, where I first encountered it, by friends of the Nào Project after his death, including the referenced poem "I Swallowed a Moon Made of Iron."

94 "Under which flag" owes a debt to the title poem from Myung Mi Kim's collection *Under Flag* (Kelsey Street Press, 1991).